Vindicated Sports Presents:

Pro Basketball's Guideline To Success Overseas

By

Michael J. Creppy Jr.

All Rights Reserved.

This book or parts thereof may not be reproduced in any form, stored in any retrieval system, or transmitted in any form by any means—electronic, mechanical, photocopy, recording, or otherwise—without prior written permission of the publisher, except as provided by United States of America copyright law.

Every effort has been made to ensure that the content provided is accurate and helpful for the readers at publishing time. However, this is not an exhaustive treatment of the subjects. No liability is assumed for losses or damages due to the information provided.

First Edition

©Michael J. Creppy Jr.-Vindicated Sports, August 2017

Images are property of Michael J. Creppy Jr.
All other photos are of Public Domain or Royalty Free images

Book Formatting &Design:

WM Productions

Editing:

L. Elliott

Table of Contents

Bio/Introduction: 1

I. Agents: 3

II. Contracts: 9

III. Salary: 28

IV. Playing Abroad: 32

V. Game Film: 38

VI. Passports: 42

VII. Living Abroad: 50

VIII. Camps/Showcases: 56

IX. Off-Court Opportunities: 60

Words of Wisdom: 64

Be Hands On In Your Career!

Be Community Minded!

Guideline To Success Overseas

INTRODUCTION

My name is Michael J Creppy Jr. I am a 7 year professional basketball player from Silver Spring, Maryland. I have played my entire career in Europe, in countries such as Greece, Germany, Denmark, Portugal & the U.K. I decided to write this book after reflecting on the start to my career, as well as conversing with other professional basketball players.

During these introspective moments, I noticed that when I began my career, I had little to no education on how the business of professional basketball worked overseas.

I've talked to many players who prematurely gave up on pursuing their careers, and to a man, they said that if they had the information in this book, they would still be playing today. My career is very unique in that I have maneuvered the camp/showcase circuit, the USA minor league system, and made it all the way to the top divisions in Europe.

I can speak from a perspective that very few players can and the majority of the information in this book has come from the good & bad experiences I've encountered over the course of my career.

My mission with this book is to help the next group of players with the ambition of playing professional basketball overseas to be as prepared as possible to have an enjoyable and lucrative career playing the greatest game on earth.

Michael J. Creppy Jr.

Guideline To Success Overseas

I. Agents

THEY WORK FOR YOU!

You are young, eager, and unfamiliar with the international basketball market. Knowing this, agents will try to make you think they are in charge, but never forget that agents only get paid if you sign a contract and that they work for you.

NEVER GIVE MONEY TO AN AGENT!

Agents (Internationally) get paid directly from the team in which you sign. Only in the NBA are the players required to pay the agent fees. Agents only get paid after you have signed a contract. If an agent or team is asking you to pay them money for any reason, it is a scam, so end all communication with them immediately.

Guideline To Success Overseas

There are agencies all over the world (U.S., Europe, Asia, South America, Australia). Research and interview each agent before you sign. Reach out on Facebook and other social media outlets to current and former players represented by the agency, to get their firsthand accounts of their experiences with the agency. A few important questions that must be asked before signing with an agent are:

1. How many clients do they have?

You want to be with an experienced agency that has a good number of clients, but not at the expense of you being unable to receive the attention needed to sign a deal in a timely fashion. As previously stated, agents only get paid if the client signs a contract, so naturally if the agency has a good amount of high profiled players, they will dedicate the majority of their time and resources to those players. Keep that in mind while interviewing each agency.

2. How many of those clients didn't sign last season?

Just as it is important know how many clients a particular agency has, it is even more important to know how many of those players didn't sign a contract that season. One year without signing a contract, can be deadly to your career. Teams internationally will question why you didn't sign a deal the previous season, and it will make them hesitant to sign you. This is a very revealing statistic of an agency, and should not be taken lightly when determining whether or not to sign with them.

3. Which markets do they primarily work?

Guideline To Success Overseas

As will be explained in the subsequent sections, each country/market has varying levels of play as well as economic stability. Depending on your motivation (level of play, or money), you will want to sign with an agency that has strong ties and good relationships in those markets.

4. Which markets will they target for you?

Nothing is ever guaranteed. If an agent guarantees with 100% certainty they can land you a deal, that is a major red flag. No responsible agent will ever guarantee that you will obtain a contract by signing with them.

However, a good indicator of a quality agent is them guaranteeing that they will work hard to obtain you a good contract. Once your potential agent thoroughly explains their markets of expertise, you will want to know based on their experiences in those markets, how confident they are they can land you a deal.

Ask as many questions as you need to ease any concerns you have. Don't worry about annoying or badgering your agent. If you have a question, call or message them.

THEY WORK FOR YOU!

II. Contracts

Michael J. Creppy Jr.

Every contract is different from player to player. Really depends on your profile, agent, and the strength of the relationship they have with the team. All Contracts will include your salary, insurance info, amenities (housing, internet, car (optional), etc.), obligations to be fulfilled by the player, obligations to be fulfilled by the team, tax information (always paid by the team), what happens if injured, Penalties if the team pays late etc.

Your contract can also include incentives/bonuses (Points bonus, rebounds bonus, blocks bonus, wins bonus, playoff bonus, Meals, etc.) Always ask your agent to try and negotiate these bonuses into your contract.

CONTRACT EXAMPLE:

In the town of ATHENS, Greece on January 2, 2013 ASSEMBLED

Guideline To Success Overseas

On the one side

Mr. Jones, representing Euro basketball team (hereinafter "the Club"), entity domiciled in the city Athens, Greece

On the other side

Mr. Michael J. Creppy Jr., basketball Player (hereinafter "the Player"), of American nationality.

Reciprocally recognize to each other the necessary legal capacity to oblige themselves and to contract, in the respective status in which that intervene, freely and spontaneously,

DECLARE

That Jones basketball team is interested in contracting the services of Mr. Michael J. Creppy Jr.

Michael J. Creppy Jr.

That having arrived to an agreement referring to the rendering of services indicated on the previous record, both parties commonly agree on the following

COVENANTS

FIRST- Mr. Michael J. Creppy Jr. engages himself to fulfill his activities as a basketball Player in the official competitions and friendly tournaments in which the Club may take part during the 2012-2013 basketball seasons, as well as in the happenings and matches of "All-Stars" for which he may be selected. The tenants of this agreement is from the following day of the signing of this contract, until five (5) days after the last game of the official competition of the 2012-2013 season, being understood that once this time has passed, Player shall be free to leave the city whenever he finds it appropriate.

Guideline To Success Overseas

SECOND- To the effects of what is foreseen in the first section the Player will have to:

Train in the frame of the technical structure of the Club and take care of his good physical condition in order to obtain the best possible performance in his activity.

Use the clothing and sporting material provided by the Club. Except in the case of basketball shoes, the Player may wear any basketball shoes by any sponsor for official Club games and events.

Observe the regulations and internal rules of the Club. Rules will be given to the Player in English upon arrival.

THlRD-The Club will pay the Player for his services, the amount euro (hereinafter USO) net Per Month of all Greek taxes, from the date of this contract through the end of 2012-13 season as follows:

xxxxEuro NET after the medical and before the first game.

Signed: --
Player

Agent: --
Club

And after 2 May for every day who the player stays in the club, he will get xxx euro net per day

BONUS- 2012-13 SEASONS - BONUSES ARE NET OF ALL GREEK TAXES

Mr. Michael J. Creppy Jr. will receive the following bonuses: Club will pay highest bonus earned in each section.

Guideline To Success Overseas

PLAYOFF SEASON BONUS

If the Club gets in 6 position in the regular season, the player will get xxx USD net.

If the club stays in division, the player he will get xxx USD.

ALL BONUSES ARE CUMULATIVE AND ARE PAID WITHIN I5 DAYS OF EARNING THEM

FOURTH- In each contract year, the Club will provide the Player, free of charge, with one (1) Roundtrip airplane tickets (economy class) from his town of origin in the USA to his residence in Greece. The Club agrees to pay up to the sum of $xxx USD each way toward the cost of shipping Player's personal items from the USA to

Greece and back at the beginning and end of the term.

The Club will also provide the Player with housing in good conditions - at least a one bedroom apartment, whilst the contract is in force. The apartment shall be fully furnished and equipped with all the necessary conveniences (color TV, DVD, washer, dryer, internet access, etc.). The apartment and its conditions shall be subject to Player's approval. The Club will pay all utilities, internet fees. The apartment will have a telephone installed. However, the repercussions of damages to the apartment by the Player, the telephone bill, and the maintenance of the car will be at his charge. Also 2 meals per day until the end of the season.

FIFTH- The Club guarantees to the Player and his family free medical, health and dental coverage by the services of the

Guideline To Success Overseas

same Club, or in any case, by the services concerted with third parties. Plastic surgery is not included.

SIXTH - The Player accepts and pledges to fulfill the norms that regulate the competitions in which the Club may participate.

SEVENTH- In regards to all salary monies payable to the Player, the termination or suspension of this contract by the Club on account of an injury, illness, or disability suffered or sustained by the Player, or on account of the Player's failure to exhibit sufficient skill, shall in no way affect the Player's right to receive the sums payable under this contract at such times as the sums become due.

EIGHTH- The Player could be asked while this contract is in force, to take drug and alcohol tests at any time required by the Club.

    Signed:
    Player:
    Agent:
    Club:

NINTH-The Player declares to be in possession of the documents required by the legislation regulating the working conditions for foreigners in Greece. In case, the Player must apply for the working and resident pemlit in Greece, the Player will provide the Club with all the necessary documents to obtain such permit. It is Club's responsibility to report and submit all of Player's documents for appropriate permits and working visas.

TENTH-Any dispute arising from or related to the present contract shat I be submitted to the FJBA Arbitral Tribunal

Guideline To Success Overseas

(FAT) in Geneva, Switzerland and shall be resolved in accordance with the FAT Arbitration Rules by a single arbitrator appointed by the FAT President. The seat of the arbitration shall be Geneva, Switzerland. The arbitration shall be governed by Chapter 12 of the Swiss Act on Private International Law (PIL), irrespective of the parties' domicile. The language of the arbitration shall be English. The arbitrator shall decide the dispute ex aequo et bono.

ELEVENTH- If the Club does not make any payment due to the Player and or Agents on the date called for under this contract, the Club shall pay the Player or the agents an additional € xxx per day until such amount due is received by the Player or by the Agents. If such original amount owed is not paid within twenty-five (25) days, Player will not be required to practice or play basketball for the team until the payment is received, but the obligations of the Club shall continue.

In addition, if any scheduled payment is not received by the Player within 30 (thirty) days of the due date, the Player's performance obligations shall cease, Player shall be free to leave Greece with his FIBA letter of Clearance to play basketball anywhere in the world Player chooses, but the duties and liabilities of Club under this Agreement shall continue in full force and effect.

TWELTH- When due to the unsporting behavior of the Player that was sanctioned with a fine by the jurisdictional federative institutions, the Club will impute its amount to the Player. If due to the fine the Player cannot take place in official games for more than one month, the Club could then rescind the contract unilaterally.

Guideline To Success Overseas

THIRTEENTH- The Player pledges himself, while the present contract is neither in force, not to negotiate other contracts with third Clubs, neither personally nor through agents.

FOURTEENTH- Upon termination of this Agreement, Player shall be a free agent in accordance to ULEB's regulations.

FIFTEENTH- The Club agrees to pay the Agent's fee to agent xxx euro net, for its services as the Player's representative, in the terms and conditions stipulated in the attached commission page which is included as an annex to the contract. This commission is considered part of the Player's Contract.

SIXTEENTH - This Agreement shall not be assigned, transferred, traded or sold in any manner to any other team anywhere in the world without the express written consent and approval of Player which may be granted or denied in his sole discretion. Upon completion or termination of this Agreement, the Club shall have no rights over or with respect to Player, and the Club will not be entitled to request or receive any payments pertaining to the Player playing basketball anywhere in the world in accordance with ULEB and FIBA regulations.

SEVENTEENTH - Club agrees that any extension or modification of this Agreement, or future agreements between the Player and the Club must be negotiated through the Player's Representative.

EIGHTEENTH - This Contract may be executed in counterparts, each of which shall constitute ar. original but all together shall constitute one and the same Contract. Facsimile copies of the signed Contract may be transmitted between the parties hereto

Guideline To Success Overseas

and a facsimile copy of a signed Contract shall be deemed a counterpart hereof.

NINETEENTH - TAXES   All Salary and Bonuses earned by the Player and Agents under the terms of this Agreement and its Annex will be considered net. The Club will be charged with the amount of deducted income taxes, payroll and all social security taxes from the application of the corresponding tables, according to the annual payment. Prior to his departure, Club shall provide Player with written verification of all taxes paid at an income tax rate of no less than xx%.

TWENTIETH - Guaranteed Checks and/or Bank Line of Credit: Upon Player's arrival in GREECE for the 2012/13 season, Club will give to Player's Agent, (Agent), guaranteed post-dated checks for each salary and payment and Agent's fee Payment due to the Player and Agents for the 2012/13 season. These checks will be issued and paid directly from the Television Rights or Sponsor money the Club receives.

If Club does not give guaranteed postdated checks, it may also establish a letter of credit with a bank for the Player and Agent payments, in the name of the Agent and Player. If Club does not give the guaranteed Post-dated checks or Bank line of credit to the Agent upon arrival, Player will be free to leave the Club with his FIBA letter of Clearance, but Club's obligations will continue.

TWENTY-FIRST - Injuries and diseases: In case of injury or disease, so serious to stop the normal sport activities, the club agrees to pay anyway all the salaries, bonus and amenities as above established, until the end of the contract. In the event surgery is required, Player will choose the doctor to perform the surgery and

Guideline To Success Overseas

where the surgery will be performed after 2nd opinion that is the right of the Player - all costs associated with the 2nd opinion will be paid by the Club. All rehabilitation will be conducted in Greece under the Club's and the surgeon's supervision.

The Player declares himself available to stipulate an insurance paid by the Club or the Player, upon player's preference.

TWENTY-SECOND - Any discrepancy between this Agreement in English, and any league or image contracts in other languages, executed for league or federation purposes, this Agreement will be the prevailing and controlling agreement above any other with all protections and governing language described herein.

(SIGNATURES ON FOLLOWING PAGE)

Michael J. Creppy Jr.

THIS CONTRACT IS A FULL-GUARANTEED AGREEMENT

And as a sign of agreement, endorse the present contract, in four copies in the place and date mentioned above.

Guideline To Success Overseas

Michael J. Creppy Jr.

III. Salary

Guideline To Success Overseas

DON'T FOCUS ON THE MONEY YOUR FIRST YEAR.

Be more concerned about signing to a team that will allow you to play big minutes, so you have the opportunity to put up good stats. The money will come.

I know you see current pros posting the things they buy and the trips they take on social media and it's natural to think that is what playing basketball overseas will be like from day one. What these current pros neglect to post is how they had to work to reach their current level of salary.

Very few players begin their career at the top leagues and make six figures. Unless you have NBA on your resume (Draft pick, training camp invite, etc.) you will have to start at a moderate league, prove yourself by putting up good numbers, and work your way up the ranks.

Michael J. Creppy Jr.

A huge misconception many players have is just because you have a lot of talent, and you train with high paid players, does not mean you are obligated the money they make. Your profile (Where you played, your stats, your measurements etc.) will determine your salary. Be prepared to take a low salary your rookie season. Some teams may offer you less than 1,000 euros per month, but if you put up big numbers, you can jump to 8,000 euros per month the next season. Stats are everything in International basketball.

Your stats will determine the salaries you will be offered.

Guideline To Success Overseas

IV. Playing Abroad

Guideline To Success Overseas

The style of play as it pertains to international basketball is very different than America. The game as a whole is more team oriented and less about individual players. Most offenses are predicated on ball movement and player movement. Dribbling eight times, running down the shot clock, and taking a contested shot will be frowned upon and can potentially get you cut. As you prepare to continue your basketball career overseas, watch as many games of the top teams around the world.

Teams such as CSKA Moscow (Russia), Real Madrid (Spain), and Panathaniakos (Greece) will give an adequate depiction of the style of international basketball played at the highest level. Also, watch NBA teams such as the San Antonio Spurs whose coaching staff is comprised of many international coaches and have adopted a European style offense which has made them championship contenders year after year.

Although international basketball is less about the individual player at the higher leagues, if you have to start your career at a lower league in Europe or South America, you will be expected and need to put up big numbers (points, assists, rebounds, etc.) to gain the interest of the bigger clubs with the better money.

However as I mentioned, once you make it to the higher leagues, remember most high budget clubs have multiple players that can score 20 ppg easily, so you might be required to take a lesser offensive role to help the team win at that higher level. A huge difference between pros and good players who never make it is: pros understand how to be a team player and fill a role if need be despite having the ability to do more.

Guideline To Success Overseas

The international game is a possession game. In a 48 minute NBA game, you can potentially get away with a 2-3 minute stretch of bad shots and still be in a position to win. In a 40 minute international game, a 2-3 minute stretch of poor shots and turnovers can put you in an insurmountable deficit.

Make sure your off-season training leading up to your first season overseas and each subsequent off-season is productive and filled with pick n roll drills, catch & shoot, 1-2 dribble pull ups and stepbacks with counter moves. You will do these actions the majority of each game.

Work Hard but Work Smart.

Lastly, one major FIBA rule of which all international basketball players must be aware, and that is drastically different from

Michael J. Creppy Jr.

basketball in the States, is the timeout policy. International basketball only allows for timeouts to come from the Head Coach and even after the Coach signals for a timeout, play will continue until the next dead ball. Then and only then, will the timeout be granted. So remember, while you're playing, you as a player cannot call a timeout from the floor. Having this knowledge entering your international basketball career will help expedite your adjustment process from American basketball to International Basketball.

Guideline To Success Overseas

Michael J. Creppy Jr.

V. Game Film

Guideline To Success Overseas

DON'T ADD MUSIC!

A lot of songs have copyright restrictions that make videos unplayable in other countries outside of the U.S. You might have a really sharp and professional highlight film, but if it contains restricted music, then the teams will not be able to watch one second of it. Instrumentals sometimes are ok, but to be safe, use no music. Just normal basketball game sounds from the original film.

Learn to create your own highlight film even if your college coach or agent is willing to do it for you. There are a number of user friendly programs such as: **Windows Movie Maker, Final Cut Pro, and Youtube Movie Maker** that make creating a professional highlight film simple. Learning to create your own highlight film is important because life as a professional basketball player abroad can be very nomadic, and if you play well, there might be another team with better money, interested in your services. You need to have game film from your current team readily available, so you don't miss the opportunity. Aside from having your film readily available, creating a highlight film allows yourself to be in control of the plays and content teams will scout to evaluate you.

BE HANDS ON IN YOUR CAREER!

Organize the clips in your game film by category and add variety.

1. Scoring- Catch & Shoot, Pick n Roll, Pick n Pop, transition, post ups, moving without the ball etc.

2. Defense- on the ball, off the ball.

3. Passing/Playmaking

Guideline To Success Overseas

Make sure it's easy to identify where you are on the court. Describe your team and what number you are in the title of the film, so teams know exactly who they're watching.

Ex. https://www.youtube.com/watch?v=stO2-nghZ4Q

Get your film even while playing overseas. Especially your first few seasons. Try to get each game film as soon as possible from your team and save it to your laptop, so you can put your highlight film together throughout the season and won't have to do it all at once at the end.

Michael J. Creppy Jr.

VI. Passports

Guideline To Success Overseas

American/Canadian players can play anywhere in the world and are considered imports. As are any players who don't have citizenship in the country, in which they play.

As professional basketball player overseas, having Dual Citizenship is a very important topic to discuss with members of your family. Having Dual Citizenship can drastically help your career and increase your chances of getting signed because each country is only allowed a certain number of imports.

If a team has already signed its imports, then they can still sign you because you have a passport that classifies you as a Non-Import. Ask your family if your parents or grandparents have citizenship in other countries. If they do, you are eligible to have that citizenship in addition to your U.S./Canadian passport.

NEVER GIVE UP YOUR U.S. CITIZENSHIP.

It is a very tedious and difficult process to obtain citizenship in the U.S. so under no circumstance renounce that citizenship.

NEVER PAY FOR DUAL CITIZENSHIP.

You cannot buy a passport for another country it is illegal and could result in jail time. If anybody says they can get you a passport if you pay them, it's a scam.

Each country has constant changing rules depicting the criteria a foreigner must meet before being classified as a Non-Import. Europe has the most complex. There are 3 categories for Non- Imports In Europe

Guideline To Success Overseas

(players with European, African, & Caribbean passports) These are: Bosman A, Bosman B, & Contonou.

1. Bosman A.- E.U. Countries & Switzerland (Austria, Belgium, Bulgaria, Croatia, Republic of Cyprus, Czech Republic, Denmark, Estonia, Finland, France, Germany, Greece, Hungary, Ireland, Italy, Latvia, Lithuania, Luxembourg, Malta, Netherlands, Poland, Portugal, Romania, Slovakia, Slovenia, Spain, Sweden and the UK.).

Players holding passports from these countries can play as an Import or Non-Import anywhere in the European Union & Switzerland without any restrictions. Bosman A players can also play in the Bosman B countries but there might be restrictions on the numbers allowed, depending on the country.

2. Bosman B- E.U. Countries not in E.U. (Norway, Iceland, Albania, Switzerland, Turkey, Russia, Macedonia & Montenegro.

Players holding passports from these countries can play in Bosman B countries without any restrictions. Bosman B players can also play in Bosman A countries but there might be a restriction on the number allowed, depending on the country.

3. Cotonou African & Caribbean
(Angola Anguilla, Antigua, Aruba, Bahamas, Barbados, Belize, Botswana, Burkina Faso, Burundi, Cameroon, Cape Verde, Central Africa, Chad, Cook Islands, Cuba, Dominica, Dominican Republic, Eritrea, Ethiopia, Fiji, Gabon, Gambia, Ghana, Guam, Guinea, Guinea Bissau, Guyana, Haiti, Ivory Coast, Jamaica, Kenya, Lesotho, Liberia, Macau, Madagascar, Mali, Marshall

Guideline To Success Overseas

Islands, Mauritania, Mauritius Island, Micronesia, Mozambique, Namibia, Nauru, Nigeria, Palau, Papua New Guinea, Rwanda, Saint Kitts, Saint Lucia, Saint Vincent and the Grenadines, Samoa, Senegal, Seychelles, Sierra Leone, Solomon Islands, South Africa, Sudan, Suriname, Tanzania, Tonga, Trinidad and Tobago, Turks and Caicos, Uganda, Vanuatu, Zambia, and Zimbabwe).

Contonou players can also play in some European countries, most notably Spain, France, Italy, and Switzerland.

Michael J. Creppy Jr.

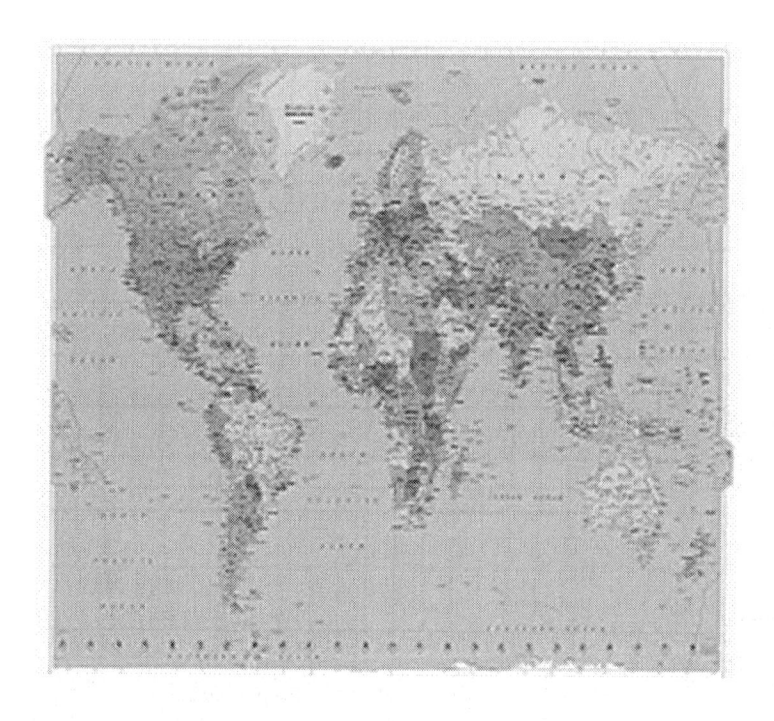

Guideline To Success Overseas

Michael J. Creppy Jr.

VII. Living Abroad

Guideline To Success Overseas

YOU ARE NOT ON VACATION, YOU ARE THERE TO WORK!

The team you play for is considered the "NBA" team for that city/town. If you go out, people will see you, tweet about what you're doing, and the team will know. If the team thinks your off court activities are affecting your play and the team's ability to win, they will terminate your contract and send you home.

International basketball is not as regulated as the NBA. Even if you have a guaranteed contract, if your team is displeased with you, they will withhold your money without hesitation leaving you only the recourse of taking them to court for a long court proceeding. So be mindful of this reality even when things are going well.

Stay professional at all times.

You can still have fun and enjoy all the luxuries that playing overseas affords you (shopping, travelling to neighboring countries/cities, learning new cultures etc.), but always remember why you are there and that basketball is your main priority.

BE PROFESSIONAL

(Despite disagreements with coaches/management & teammates)

Keep a great relationship with your teammates. You are in a foreign country, and your teammates and team personnel are the first friends you will meet. You will need them if obstacles arise. However, I encourage you to go out and make friends in the community of your city so you can get the full cultural experience and have lifelong friends outside of your team who can help you through difficult situations. Going to

Guideline To Success Overseas

local coffee shops, restaurants, malls etc. are easy ways to meet people, especially since you will be easily recognizable.

Forget your American norms and embrace your new country and city. While playing abroad, you might have to be prepared to live without basic necessities that you are accustomed too in America. Things such as a dryer, no tape before practice, no ice after practice etc. might not be provided by the team, so you will have to be resourceful, creative and patient while you adjust.

Buying your own ice, making homemade ice baths, learning to tape your own ankles, investing in a "Game Ready" machine, are all things you should be prepared to do. As I've stated multiple times, this is your career and your body. You are responsible for its maintenance so you can perform each game and remain healthy throughout the season.

Michael J. Creppy Jr.

The quicker you realize you are no longer in America and embrace your new culture, the more successful, and enjoyable your experience playing abroad will be

Guideline To Success Overseas

Michael J. Creppy Jr.

VIII. Camps/Showcases

Guideline To Success Overseas

Each year, there are an overwhelming amount agency camps and international showcases throughout the world. Some of the better showcases that have higher success rates are usually held in Las Vegas during the summer, coinciding with the NBA Summer League.

However, many camps/showcases that are held in other locations are "money grabs" with very low results of getting players signed. Many organizers of these camps/showcases prey on player's ignorance and desperation. Charging hundreds of dollars and not creating a successful environment that results in players signing contracts.

A few things to consider before deciding to pay to attend a camp or showcase are:

1. Research the camp/showcase. Ask how many players have signed deals from this showcase and how many specifically from last year's camp? If possible, ask former players who attended the camp about their experiences. Reach out to them on social media. You'll be surprised how willing fellow players are to help.

2. Indicators that the camp/showcase is more concerned about helping the players than just taking money are: if they pay for a hotel, provide meals, each game is filmed and able to be obtained.

Most guys who need to attend a camp/showcase, usually need a recent game film in an organized setting, so attending a camp/showcase that provides game film, is a wise decision.

Guideline To Success Overseas

IX. Off-Court Opportunities

Guideline To Success Overseas

As a professional basketball player, there is a perception that players receive a variety of endorsement opportunities. This is the case in the NBA. Endorsement opportunities are readily available for players in the League. This is not the case with American players overseas.

It is very rare for American players to get endorsement opportunities overseas. Much of this is due to the fact that most American players sign short term contracts with a club, making it difficult to establish a brand.

However, there are ways as an international professional basketball player to create various streams of income within the game of basketball. There are opportunities all over the world to partner with big sports brands (Nike, Adidas, etc.) to do clinics and events while they try to grow their brand through the game of basketball in designated markets around the world.

    These companies will pay for your round trip flight, pay you a lucrative salary, and you'll get to network with other businesses that can open doors to other off-court opportunities. Another opportunity that is available is sports modeling and acting. As a professional athlete, you are already in shape, so use your physique to your advantage.

    As a professional basketball player, you will be admired and revered, so Mentoring and training younger players is another business opportunity. While this can obviously generate another source of income, this endeavor will be fulfilling and a have long lasting positive impact on the kids you encounter.

Guideline To Success Overseas

TAKE THIS RESPONSIBILITY SERIOUSLY!

These are just a few examples of opportunities through the game of basketball that can generate income while you are not playing. Use the knowledge you've gained throughout your years of playing basketball, and monetize your experiences as a professional basketball player to create multiple streams of income.

Michael J. Creppy Jr.

Words of Wisdom

Guideline To Success Overseas

The world of professional basketball overseas is a wonderful opportunity to get paid traveling the world, and doing what you love. However, there is a huge responsibility once you have the title of professional basketball player attached to your name. Society will hold to a higher standard, kids will be heavily influenced by what you say, do and post on social media.

BE COMMUNITY MINDED and make sure you're using influence in a positive way. There are a lot of temptations and distractions waiting to derail your success. It is important to stay close to God and keep Christ first in your lives. If you use the lifestyle basketball has created to humbly help others and honor God, you will have a long & successful career.

Michael J. Creppy Jr.

Guideline To Success Overseas

Contact Michael J. Creppy Jr.

Facebook- Mike Creppy

Instagram- seymour_buckets14

Email- mcreppy42@gmail.com

Michael J. Creppy Jr.

Made in the USA
Columbia, SC
02 August 2019